France

Written and illustrated by Peter Maddocks
Researched by Janine Amos

Purnell

Hello – yes, it's me, Jimbo, off on a sightseeing tour of France – the land of wine, good food and the Eiffel Tower. Come on, Amanda baggage truck, get those cases on board and let's get airborne. Ready for take off, chief – fasten your seat belts everybody.

As we travel through France, I'll tell you about all the wonderful things the French have to offer besides good food and wine – we can even learn to say a few French words...

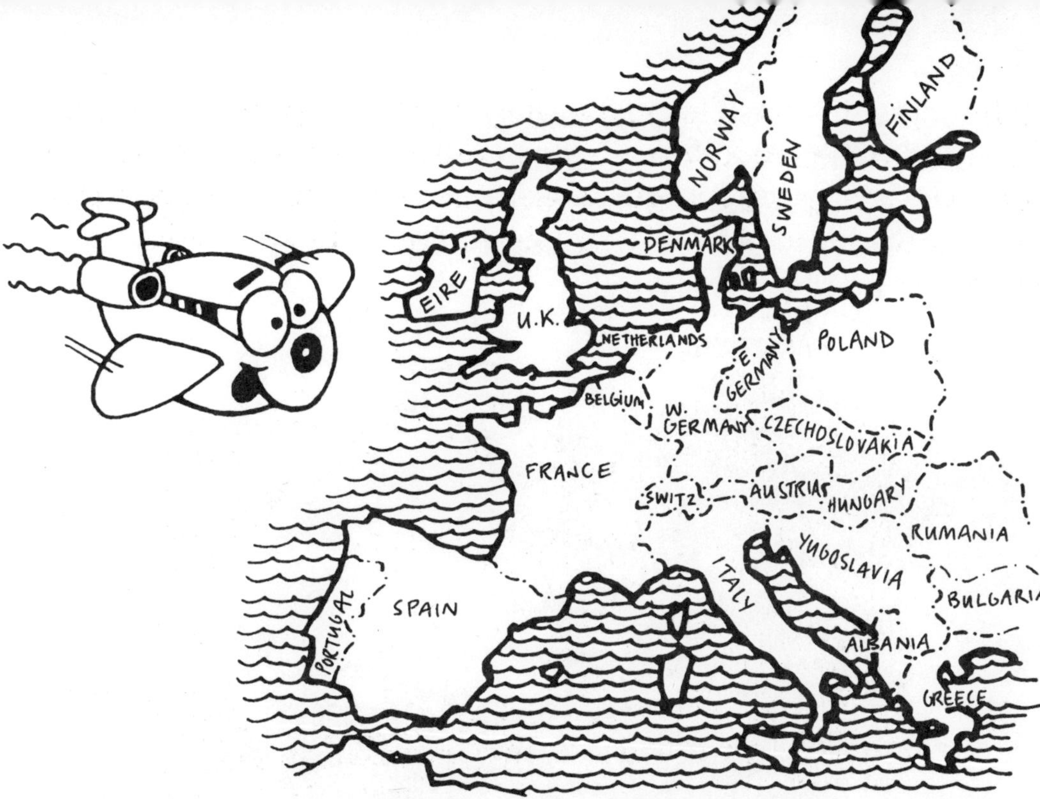

'Bye, Amanda. 'Bye, Phil. France – here we come!

Look at your map of Europe while the stewardess brings you all a snack. See how big France is on your map? In about one hour's time we'll land and go to Rouen.

Now then you lot, off you go and take a look around the town of Rouen and the market. You might see the spot in the centre of town where Joan of Arc was burnt as a witch. And you can still visit the tower where she was kept prisoner. Behave yourselves, you don't want to end up the same way!

Try getting your tongue around some French words. These are the names of French shops.
Une boulangerie – a baker's.
Une boucherie – a butcher's.
Une épicerie – a grocer's.
That's it, keep going.
Une pâtisserie – a cake shop.
And *un café* – one orange juice please.
Merci – thank you.

French money looks like this, and goes just as quickly as English money.
Come on you lot, it's time to take off again!

Now, if you'll look at your map on pages 12 and 13, you'll find we're passing over Normandy. This is famous for its cathedrals and creamy cheese. I've had a cheese and pickle sandwich but never a cheese and cathedral one – I bet it plays havoc with your teeth!

Anyway, you could stand and eat it while you study the Bayeux Tapestry. That's the story of England's invasion by William the Conquerer. It's in a place called Bayeux. Well, it would be!

Further on, there is a big rock sticking out of marshy, shallow waters on the coast. Look, there it is down there – it's a wonderful monastery called Mont Saint Michel, built by monks hundreds of years ago. You can't miss it, can you? There's a narrow strip of road leading to it across the marshes.

Here we are over Saint Malo, another seaside town. Look, there are some children playing France's favourite game, *boules*.

The game is good fun and it's so easy you can carry a set of boules around with you and play it anywhere. It's like a heavyweight game of marbles really...

French children work very hard at school – not like you lot. They have Wednesdays off from school in France, but they have to go in on Saturday mornings – boo! But they do have very long summer holidays – two and a half months – hooray! *Vive la France...*

The French love seafood – mussels cooked in wine is called *moules marinières*. But whatever you call it, it's still delicious!

That's the River Loire down there. It's France's longest river and along its banks you'll find lots of huge castles – the French word is *châteaux* – with dungeons. Hundreds of years ago they belonged to kings and barons. That one down there is the Château of Chenonceaux, once the home of King François I – whoever he was!

Hang on kids, we're coming to Nantes. It's quite a large town so I'd better gain height – we don't want to wake up all the babies having their afternoon nap. That reminds me, I'm hungry and it's way past my lunch time...

One thing the French do like is to have a picnic, with lots of lovely cheese and their lovely crunchy bread. There are great, long bread sticks, called *baguettes* in French – ideal for fencing in the playground. My favourite is their cheese – which they call *fromage* – and specially the *fromage de chèvre*. That's goat's cheese and it's delicious. Ooh, go on, taste some, scrumptious!

This map shows you our journey through France.

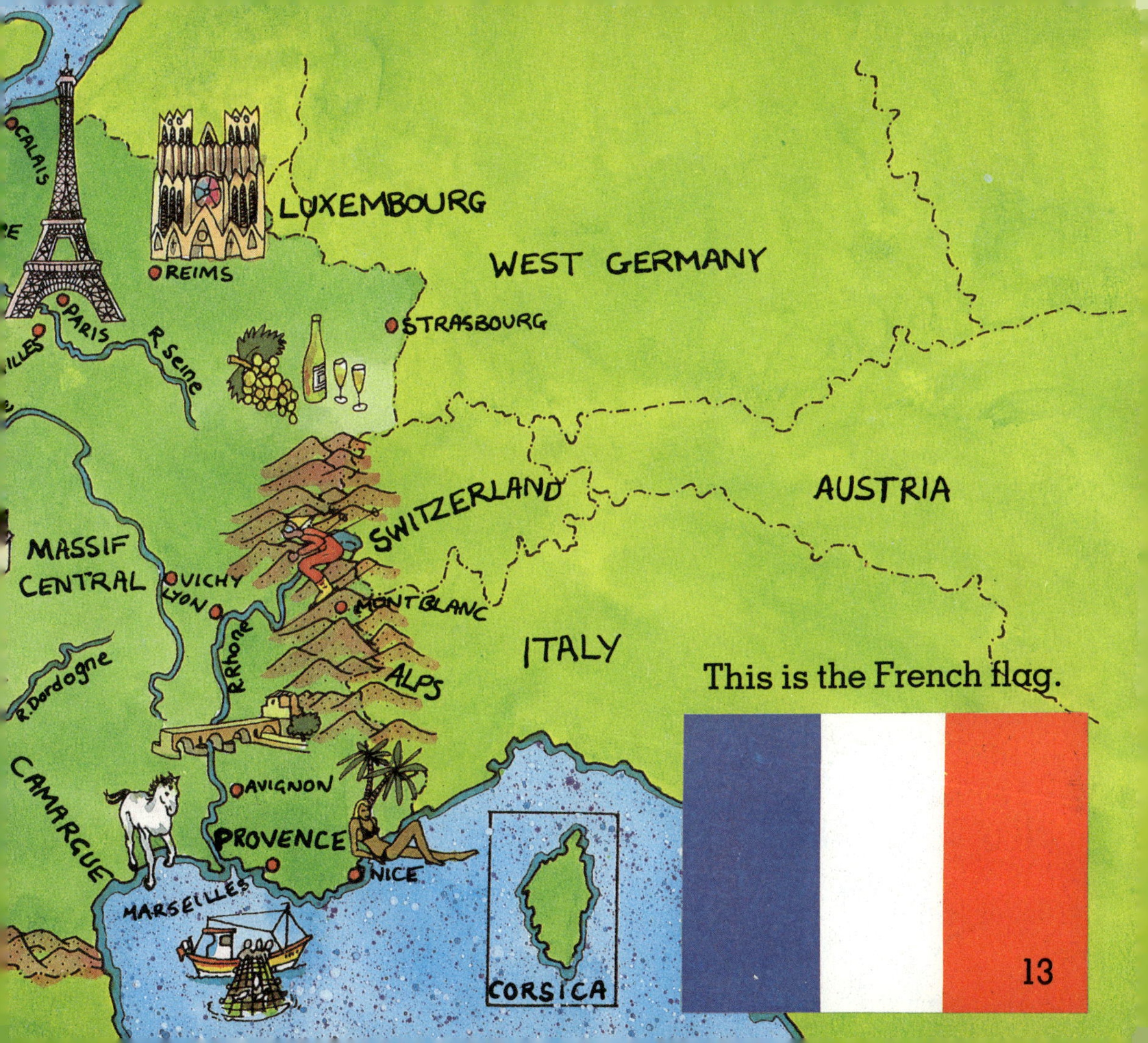

This is the French flag.

Now here's a place that goes well with cheese. It's called Bordeaux and is a beautiful old town in an area where a lot of lovely wine comes from. The wine is shipped out from here – a very busy port in this part of France.

Wine is very popular and cheap, and even young children drink a little wine at meal times – maybe that's why they have Wednesdays off from school? (Chuckle!)

Of course you know that wine is made from grapes grown in a vineyard. People pick the grapes and squeeze all the juice out. (Have you seen pictures of people treading the grapes with their feet? Well, that's the old-fashioned way of doing it, now there are machines.)

Anyway, the juice is stored in huge vats until it's ready to put into those green bottles ready to drink – cheers!

We're over Marseilles on the south coast of France. It's France's largest port, and is a busy, noisy place. You can stand on the dockside and look out to the island of the Château d'If. In a book by Alexandre Dumas, that's where the Count of Monte Cristo was imprisoned.

Further on we pass the French Riviera and Nice, which is one of France's favourite holiday places.

There is a lot to see around Nice, such as the market, and the harbour. There's the Musée Matisse, too, a museum showing work by the famous French painter Henri Matisse. And in the nearby city of Grasse, most French perfumes are made. Mmm! Smells delicious!

On Shrove Tuesday in Nice there is a carnival. Floats covered with flowers move through the town. In the evening a huge dummy is burnt on a bonfire – reminds me of something English!

Oh great, now we're crossing the high Alps. Look, there's Mont Blanc. It's more than 4800 metres high – the highest mountain in Europe. And did you know there's a tunnel under the mountain linking France and Italy?

Give me the open skies any day. Oh, look, there're some skiers zooming on their way down the mountainside – I wish I could do that, it must be great fun.

Towards the centre of France is a part called the Auvergne. It is known for its mountains, and green valleys with blue lakes. Waterskiing, riding, and sailing are very popular here.

And as if that's not healthy enough, drinking the famous water at Vichy, in the Auvergne, is supposed to keep you healthy!

And here we are in Paris, the capital of France, with its wide, tree-lined streets and lots of famous buildings. Take a pleasure boat called a *bateau mouche* (it looks a bit like a floating bus) and see Paris from the River Seine. The river runs through the city past the cathedral of Notre Dame, one of Europe's most beautiful cathedrals.

And don't forget to pop into the Musée du Louvre and say hello to the smiling Mona Lisa by Leonardo Da Vinci. She's always pleased to see you!

You can't miss the Eiffel Tower – it's a famous landmark. It was built in 1889 and is over 300 metres high. If you manage to climb up the 2710 steps to the top, they say you can see for about fifty kilometres in every direction. We can see more than that from up here, can't we? And we don't have to climb all those steps!

Montmartre is a very lively part of Paris, full of painters and cats. There's even a street called the Rue du Chat qui Pêche – the street of the fishing cat!

Everywhere you go in Paris there are lively restaurants and cafés where you can sit looking on to the street, watching the world go by. Cafés are where French people meet their friends and eat snacks of ham and cheese called *un croque-monsieur*. Or you could try a pancake – *une crêpe* – it's lovely!

The 14th July is Bastille Day, a national holiday for all of France. On this day in 1789 the people won their freedom from the king – and they all go bonkers dancing and singing in the streets, with carnival parades and huge firework displays that light up the evening sky.

Well, that's about it for this tour. I hope you all had a good time! Permission to land please, chief. *Au revoir*, everyone. Goodbye!

Index

Alps 13, 18
Bastille Day 23
Bayeux 6, 12
Bordeaux 12, 14
Boules 8
Châteaux 10
French language 5, 10, 11, 22
French Riviera 16
Joan of Arc 4
Loire Valley 10, 11
Marseilles 13, 16
Money 5
Mont Blanc 13, 18
Mont Saint Michel 7, 12
Moules marinières 9
Nantes 10, 12
Nice 13, 17
Paris 13, 20, 21
Rouen 4, 12
River Seine 13, 20
Saint Malo 8, 12
School 9
Shops 5
Vichy 13, 19
Wine 14, 15